www.finishinglinepress.com

Ear to the Ground

POETRY OF LIFE IN THE SANDHILLS OF COLORADO

poems by

Harriet Stratton

Finishing Line Press
Georgetown, Kentucky

Ear to the Ground

POETRY OF LIFE IN THE SANDHILLS OF COLORADO

ACKNOWLEDGMENTS

My gratitude to the editors of these publications in which the following
poems have appeared, some in other versions or with different titles:

Slippery Elm Literary Journal: "When We Were Horses"
Pilgrimage Magazine: "Burn Barrell," "Taking Leave"
Podcast: Burning Bright: "While Making Fence with My Father"
Passager Journal: "While Making Fence with My Father"
Windward Review: "Ear to the Ground"
An Uncertain Age: "The Anchor," "New Year's Day"
Poetry Society of Colorado prize winners: "Drawing from Memory", "What's
Between Us"
Secrets, Rumors and Lies: "Caught in Amber," grateful to editors of Anhinga
Press to be nominated for a 2023 Pushcart Prize

Publisher: Leah Huete de Maines
Editor: Christen Kincaid
Cover Art: Harriet Stratton
Author Photo: Harriet Stratton
Cover Design: HR Hegnauer

Order online: www.finishinglinepress.com
also available on amazon.com

Author inquiries and mail orders:
Finishing Line Press
PO Box 1626
Georgetown, Kentucky 40324
USA

Contents

The past isn't over until we understand it.
—Lawrence Raab

I

What I Can Tell You

I troubled over the approach—how to tickle
individual threads from a tangled mesh—
where to start, how to proceed—

like a weaver? warping the loom?
interleaving colored strands of remembrance
into patterns on whole cloth? Maybe—

but I'm not a weaver—more like an old singer
never sure of her voice. I project a few words—
to see if the electrons vibrate—do they orbit

like planets circle the sun? Theoreticians say
it's impossible to track electrons, that an orbit
is less fixed path than a cloud of possible positions

and there's the line that I hope might guide you
through dusky layers of a sandhill landscape
before the radiant orb of recollection sets.

Ear to the Ground

From the window seat, I can see all
ten thousand acres of the family ranch,
our winged shadow skims the treeless plain,
the gravel road that used to take me home.

In the pasture, switchgrass whorled flat
by bedding antelope bids me lie down.
On a clean sheet of sand, I rest my head,
lay a weary ear to the ground.

Buffalo grass curls, big bluestem flags
over deeply dropped roots, anchor
against blows of the wind. I can hear
grass grow, rootlets pulse and dig,

sands scuttle up-ridge to repose, only
to avalanche grain by grain, downwind.
In the present, progress sounds like a hiss
while in past tense, these sandhills whisper

phrases and names and places I miss.
A sudden gust lifts me, spins me around
as if the broom of time, itself, had come
to sweep my imprint from this ground.

How to Listen

Mule deer tilts her head,
swivels soft slipper ears,
inquires of the breeze,
the rustle in the grass.

Eyes, full contact, do not waver,
Eyes, too, listen, do not blink.
She gives herself to the present,
the story of now.

On the five-wire fence, larks
sit like grace notes, ready.
Ready for the downbeat
of the chorus at dawn.

Re-set to silent. Forget
what, so far, you've done.
It's not nothing but
fine-tune your ear
to hear what's to come.

Burn Barrel

Take the brown paper bag
from the kitchen waste basket,
the trash, garbage, refuse of the day,

carry it out beyond the quonset
to an open fifty-five-gallon drum.
Strike a match, tip it to a raw edge,

watch it singe and bloom a tulip
of flame. Smoke curls, sparks fly up
through a colorless cousin of sky

here below the wide-open wind-
blown freedom of heaven.
Dad always said, *If I taught you kids*

anything, I taught you how to work
which I never really understood
but this little job was a blessing.

I'll bet everyone overstays
their private turn at the burn barrel,
takes two steps back to contemplate

ranch-land escape into half-light,
yip and howl back at the coyotes
between yucca and brushes of sage.

I stand late by that dying altar of ash,
shake the can to a final flare
that momentarily lights the dark.

What's Between Us

A partly open barn door, redolent dark,
large-bodied animals, smell of fresh hay.
The guernsey tongues her oats.

Father plants the one-legged stool. Pressing
his forehead to fawn-colored flank, he squats,
blows warmth into the cup of his hands

before he starts to milk. The first white stream
rings the bucket like a bell.
On the fringe of a bare bulb's light, Old Paint

stands sleeping. I nuzzle under
the velvet of his breath. Rafters peak
above us, enfold us like prayer...

Abruptly, Father stands, raises
the silver pail, pours off the froth
to a congregation of cats. Trolling

the gloom with the hook of his smile,
he catches my eye, jerks his chin—beckons
come, take hold of the bucket's bail.

The sun rises higher on our way to the house.
We walk on the heels of a shadow that seems
to stretch forever ahead—two figures
joined by what they carry between them.

While Making Fence with My Father

I carry the red Hills Bros coffee can
of u-shaped fence staples which he picks
to nail barbed wire to each creosote post.

On the tailgate, we eat a sandwich.
He uncorks his thermos, I kneel in the sand
sifting silk through nine-year-old fingers.

That's how I find the tiny shell—so far
from any sea. I raise it to my father's smile.
He sweeps his arm across the prairie...

This was all underwater—far as you can see.
You're sitting at the far edge of history—
on the bed of a great ancient sea.

Something stirred in me then, like a root
reaching a depth below time. I think
I began to feel how it is to think...

as if a camera that had focused on me
backed away and through the lens, young dad
and the blue pickup appeared as an island

in the endless waves of grass... and I,
but a grain on the shore of the familiar...
lapped by an ocean of all there is yet to know.

Rancher Talks to His Daughter about Sex

At age thirteen, checking the pastures
had become routine. He needed
someone to let the wire gates down;
truck tires tracked over sharp barbs and
I closed the opening after he drove through.
We'd come to observe the herd of heifers

graze what grew between prickly pears of cactus,
windmills wheeling water from aquifers below.
Pronghorn, coyotes, burrowing owls.
Buntings larking over nests on the ground
meant it was time for breeding stock
to be trailered in and turned out.

From the cab of the pickup we watched
a slobbering big-shouldered bull bellow
and lumber up onto the hips of a cow.
Father tipped his hat back off his brow,
and eyes intent on the field ahead, said
Someday, that's going to happen to you, too.

To the Driver on Interstate 76

By now you may have noticed that
                the open range of Colorado sandhills
has no trees… so as you speed cross country
                you'll likely find little interest in
undulating hills of sagebrush and short grass
                layering to a horizon that each
morning trampolines a burning ball of gas
                through clouds of time and space.

Your attention will be drawn
                to the other side of the highway
the glint and glide of white birds
                that patrol a sizable blur of blue. They're pelicans,
which, I know, screams incongruity
                in an arid landscape but there's plenty of trees
lakeside—all leaning away—their posture
                even in the absence of wind.

If you turn your head for a sidelong look
                across the plain, you might begin to feel
naked…and not sexy naked but
                'for god's sake cover yourself' naked
which is what I want to tell you about
                growing up here—being exposed—
how the only place to hide
                is in the haze of distance

and how once you finally get the hang
                of being vulnerable, it becomes
comfortable—like washed denim, a jeans jacket
                you begin to wear collar snapped-up—
wear and wear and wear out—in search of words
                that stand out in the fields of memory
innumerable like the leaves of grass
                that wave and wave and wave you on.

Sweet Sixteen Birthday Present

It was a saddle
displayed on its tree in the living room
red bow stuck on the horn;
the leather cantle carved with roses
marked it as a seat for a woman
or a girl who once loved horses.

But I liked to ride bareback. Always had.

The buckles gleamed;
the glint of what dangled made it seem
as if the saddle had been delivered
to cinch me down, tame me, break
the wild blue horse inside
that someday soon would fly me away.

Caught in Amber

Back when I was new and alive with the buzz of bumble bee sex—
even saying 'sex' felt like a sin. Silence surrounded that pleasure
with panes of plate glass. I was left outside, forever looking in.
Pills were for married women with doctors—contraband for girls.

Freshman year, a childhood friend ends her life with a leap
out the window of the first high-rise dorm on campus. Rumor
was—love, a Mexican guy, parents who would never approve.
I knew what drove her over the ledge, but not my secret to tell.

The next spring, I flew with my roommate to El Paso, a slim system
of friendly support. There, the man who was to drive her across the border
insisted she see el medico alone. I was to wait. Black flies beat
against a dirty window—a desperate staccato for her to be returned.

When I miss my period, suddenly I'm 'caught' in police spot-lights,
the tick of a knot tightening to dread. The word for what I want—
like dry ice on my tongue. Someone knows someone who knows
a doctor with no name. Word is he does D&Cs here in town.

Brick office building, park in back. At 5 o'clock a knob-less door opens,
the eyes above the mask—a floor of flat water. Before I know it, it's done.
Someone says…*it's illegal. No one is to know.* I'm left to lift legs
out of stirrups, clean myself up. With no further word, I let myself out.

After: a baritone in my belly lows like a cow calling her calf. I spit
what should not be spoken into dark clouds of thought. To protect a doctor
and—let's be honest—hide my shame, I embrace silence and accept
the burden of a secret. Coiling inside, it is, itself, an unwanted growth.

I want to forget until I start to forget. At an estate sale, I impulse-buy
an amber nugget—not for the prehistoric gnat—but the radiance—
honey-gold—like venom, compressed. Silence preserved.
To this day, a very few friends… no one in my family knows.

Now, I've reached the age of forgetting… and accounting—the kind
that happens with unaccounted-for time. Frayed skirts of rain clouds
sweep the valley and let go… all I've held hidden…words left unsaid…
Did I keep a secret—or did the secrets keep me?

Uncommon Ground

Four days after Dad died, his mail-in ballot was delivered
and lay unopened like an unpaid bill. Relieved that his suffering
was over, I was glad he'd not cast his vote.

I'd shuffled through life's deck long enough to know
the sorrowful face cards would inevitably turn up
so why when they're dealt is it such a surprise?

In the scenario that followed, Dad's vote was not required,
beating the odds, his candidate won. Shock shook me naked
and took me to bed, a bed of gravel, gravel on fire.

Our common path diverged in the weeds of politics.
1968. 'George Wallace For President,' my first X in the box
cancelled his vote for the candidate of segregation.

Over the arc of our lives, we circled the topic of political
parties. He said there was only one other Democrat
in the family and maybe I'd caught that cold from them.

We showed our teeth in smiles when we met, pressed lips
to each other's cheeks to part. We couldn't really talk
but didn't want the conversation to end. Now, I see

no matter the distance, I live in his country. I'm the ballot
mailed from his address. His voice second-guesses
my convictions, he's the reason I will never not vote.

Some Tips on Remembering

Don't forget to forget.
     Let the grit go, let it scatter
     like sand. Let it grind itself fine
     under gravities, depravities of time.

When you must, remember slant.
     Wear recollection like an old linen shirt,
     that slipped its buttonholes to expose
     more skin than you had guts to acknowledge.

Reassess your lonesomeness.
     Consider putting it on an sliding scale.
     And regrets—keep them pliable like clay
     uncoiled, not yet fired to a ware like stone.

Still, I wish we could fire a kiln hot enough to re-forge
     certain memories, bend the arc of an angry hand,
     blunt the blade of a bitter tongue, leave us
     to soak in the white heat that remains.

Drawing from Memory

I delight in rendering the details, double-dutch
door, hand-forged hasp, whittled pine pin
in the latch, but I fail to notice until I raise

my mind's eye back to the big picture
how the barn wall skews to the side, and that
the gambrel roof tips like a farm hand's hat.

Perspective lines look to have run rogue
to dodge the demands of the vanishing point.
My hand curls to crumple the sketch until

a finger twitch hooks the loop on the pant-leg
of my grandfather's overalls, and I'm swung
like a curtain on the length of his stride, hung

on the thin wire of his smile. A high pitch yodel
reels in chickens as if on a line cast by the
rustle of ears of corn stripped from their stalks.

Mother remembers bundling sheaves into shocks
with her father, still talks of the flood of '38—
how the water rose as they hurried hens and chicks

and the collie up the steep ladder to the loft—
how the sweet smell of milk cows and hay sailed
them through that wet weeping sleep like an ark.

Found memories, I'll keep safe when I re-mark
the long brown sound of that receding river—
wild asparagus rocketing up through the dark.

"...staying on the right side of the grass."
—Doug Stratton

II

Taking Leave

His lids droop, his head lolls
like it could roll off the eaves
of his paint-peeled barn,

shelter for the milk cow,
the sweet smell of hay,
his last good horse.

Now he rides his lift chair
and sits and sits, forgets
the way to the bathroom,

a transparent tube slithers
across a path strewn with pills
like seeds in winter fallow,

pulls the TV screen close to buy
a vowel or rerun *Little House
on the Prairie* and once a week

the livestock auction where cattle sell
for pennies a pound profit ...*if
they can make their weight,* he winks.

The last time we drive by his pastures
he nods at the green macular haze,
the dark dash of creosote fence posts

pass in rhythm like the beat of a heart.
Buffalo grasslands fold and unfold
in front and around the old Caddie

and now, so quickly it seems, behind.
... *pretty good ole ranch,* he says
as if putting the old dog down.

In Memory of the Rancher and his Grindstone

Not uncle or cousin,
not grandfather or big brother
but an old bachelor neighbor

sits in the dark cave of his room,
the cave of his heart,
the cave of his small grey house.

He sits and sits, stares out his open door.
Outside the land is the story,
a story telling itself.

Trees turn their leaves, fall into Fall.
Flies fiddle tiny strings, fly as if casting a net
to catch us in their sonorous trap.

The old man cradles his shotgun,
he'll shoot the damn flies right through his screen,
plug the tears with a bit of t.p.

An implement parked in the shade out back
looks like a child's tricycle
but when I mount the seat,

push the pedals with childish feet,
its front wheel squeals and rolls
but does not move me forward.

What turned was a heavy circle of stone,
he said it whets pitchforks to a point,
grinds meal from the bone.

Like the stone, he looked rough,
pockmarked and pale as if he, himself
had been ground, made tough.

Waiting

An Ebenezer resident notices Dad's chair
empty at the lunch table, hears the highway noise,
remarks on how it comes, how it goes.

…maybe he's out for an appointment, she says
sensing the shaggy crawl of impending absence
slink like a bad dog past security.

She works her walker down to his room
How's it going in there…? leaves half a jar
of blackberry jam to the silence inside.

Marooned in the recliner, he elevates sausage legs,
wounds weep, oxygen mechanically pumps
to support his every breath.

> Across town, in my motel dreams, a soft animal
> rubs back and forth at a complex human seam
> that looms larger, longer, louder…. fades
> to black exhalation like diesel exhaust.

> A figure reclines in a rowboat,
> becalmed offshore.

On the drive back to the facility,
a black fly bumps against
the constraint of the windshield,
as if eager to get on with its last day.

A coal train stirs on the siding, rattles
the linkage, wails at the crossing.

> *…staying on the right side of the grass* he says
> when we ask how he's getting along.

Grounded in His Field

A man, plaid shirt, Levis, still tall,
salt and pepper hair, stands
as if on a solid surface,
grounded in his field of knowledge.
He was walking forward but now has stopped.
He's come to the point of the fulcrum
damned if you do, damned if you don't.
Caught up in the act of being ground
by the slow forces of the day to day,
the give and take, year after year
of living, family living.
Working. Working the ranch his whole life
to pass the baton to a fourth generation.
Will he ever be ready to relinquish
what he wants his family to have?

Notes

As a painter, I think of ground
                     as a surface,
ground as a substance
                     to prepare the substrate,
ground sustains the image
                     while applying paint.

Dad would think of ground
as an electrical circuit,
our conductor
to the earth.

The Saami vision: ground as a mirror-line,

         where the feet of the living who walk upright
                  touch
        the feet of the dead who walk upside down

Losing Ground

The man in the dream turns
toward the pickup's low beam
walks in the direction
from which he came
as if there was still a chance
to catch up with his old life.

The going slows, grows unstable
through a drift of blow sand;
he struggles, begins to sense he's lost
the groundline, knows
he's losing ground.

Contours blur on the canvas,
edges slowly dissolve.
A delicate shred of cloud stirs
a quiet breeze.

In the Spirit House

Deep in the body's hearth
a fire smolders, chokes on knots
and damp gnarls of ire,
seethes into the ear of pain.

When a blown breath
cools the swelter off his neck,
whispers *forgive them* into
the labyrinth of his ear,

racks of resentment spark
and burn like fury. Fumes
wave like festival flags
going up the flue in smoke.

Relatives

A year after scattering Dad's ashes, we drive up pasture
toward the rock outcrop that looks like earth's vertebrae ledged
between shoulders of khaki hills. This is our memorial
ground of family greats, grands and good ranch dogs. Wedged
between boulders, we find the Scotch bottle that along with the skirl
of the bagpipe fueled our eulogies. Ash grits and grace notes whirled
over the prairie and now the wind swirls it all back into our face.
Below a sentinel rock, we find a windbreak where rippled sand
reveals a broken spearhead, a knife-edged chunk of chert. In hand,
it works a weight of wonder gesturing past the past to the people
who knapped the point and sheltered right where we sit. Overhead,
it's thundering like buffalo herding clouds of kindreds to join us
here where we are relatives, not in time, not in blood but in place.

Down to Earth

When the Piper Cub ran out of fuel,
he figured to quickly land
what had become a glider;
he circled back, downed it hard,
bounced, caught a wing.

When he pulled himself out
his mouth was full of blood,
he let himself fall further
into the arms of gravity,
down to solid earth.

When he heard the pulse
that ran through him,
he listened below, around, above.
He said, that day, he heard
the thrum that makes of us all—one.

The best still lifes have emptiness.
—Ron Padgett

III

Still Life with Cow Skull and Leather Gloves

Calf skin work gloves, a pair; finger stitches undone,
lifeline stretched, permanently creased, disembodied
like an empty cast, palm up or palm down, captures
in stop action the everyday grip, the slip of absent hands.

> A coil of baling wire, bracelet shaped, rusty
> reminder that when things break down
> *(you better believe it, things will break down)*
> you'll be ready with a quick fix.

Cow skull,
Hereford or White-faced Angus,
(reminder of hybrid vigor)

> Headache bar—a small steel bludgeon,
> *(keep this under your seat*
> *where you can reach it right quick)*

Stetson, dress hat: sweat stained hatband
impressed his untanned brow
so that after sweeping off his hat
he seemed to glow under the light of a halo

> 5 Lazy S fancy belt buckle,
> polished to gold by an overhang
> of flannel-shirted belly.

In front of the easel, brush in hand, I study the set-up.
Moment to moment, my eyes change direction.
Verbs enact the work of building:

> —scan for color keys among the objects
> —scrub a tone onto the canvas
> —wash in a shade of negative space
> —mix a color on the palette
> —dab a pixel of highlight
> —stroke a fluid edge
> —brush on a shape of shadow

An image has yet to emerge
as if memory were in a state of perpetual change.

No More Than a Serpentine Memory

On a flank of the prairie, in a draw that holds
no more than a serpentine memory of water,
stands an old ranch house, beyond remembrance
of color, windows vacant like downcast eyes,
the front door hanging open like an invitation

nothing but wind-blown sand accepts. Eaves drop
into the silence of a teacup's cracked lip,
a crumpled pie pan serves only rust, cement
steps skew toward the sole of a toddler's shoe,
a blank page protrudes from a tomb of dust.

No one sees winter blow shingles from the roof.
Square nails creak and bow, lose their heads
and like a thumb zipping down the keyboard
century-old walls give way, tear from square,
rip and fold into a slow arpeggio of collapse.

No one recalls the people who lived there,
we only return to their absence the way we return
in dreams to houses where we grew up—wind
rattling the bedroom window— a sliver of moon
—maybe a slice of light under the door.

This is our social life now…

my folks say, joking their way onto the handrail
descending the stairs to the church basement.
The smell of casserole beckons us to the hot lunch
that follows our good neighbor's funeral.

This is where everybody's at—the Vets
who fired the salute, the deepest voices of the choir,
the hands who bore the coffin—all hold cups
from the 5-gallon coffee urn that the church ladies
only unpack for the really big turn-outs.

Ranchers who no longer fit their suits turn and smile.
How's it going, they say, but it's entirely superficial.
We have eyes. We're living witness to the decline,
faces losing their shine as poker players, horseshoe
tossers, lodge brothers and bowling buddies

slip one by one into the silence. Unspeakable,
it hangs over Main Street where the hardware
store stands closed; unstoppable, it seems,
the John Deere dealership's quiet; once again,
the ag community's left with one less.

Coffee's cold. A deacon begins to stack chairs,
others jump up to fold tables. Through the clatter
someone calls, *See you at the farm sale*, but most
are already out the door, now that the party's over.

Apparitions at the Farm Sale

My eyes settle on the lariat, tight
braid of rope, coiled and thong-wrapped,
still new, never loosened, never thrown,
loops never dallied round a saddle horn
or stretched straight by the weight
of a calf bawling through the branding,
never burned through leather gloves,
or callused a working hand.

But there—above the barbed wire,
the post hole digger, the handle,
there's a shadow on the wear of the wood,
the wire stretcher's ratchet dangles
over a tangle of steel posts.

Then, tracing the crease on the fender
of that blue pickup parked out back
with its ruined stock rack, big dent
in the tailgate, something happened here
to mar the bed that bad; a chain and hook
under the hay dust; ammo box, army surplus,
shovel still carries the smell of must.

I take a peek under the seat,
find the flask—emptied of anything alive,
no pity for the old ways, now dead
as the millers in the case of .22 shells, intact;
the ache of grief so sharp it could
make the pitted windshield crack.

Knowing Your Place

I might have the notion of a ghost conversation as I open the gate
behind the house. *About what?* my outer voice might ask,
eyes narrow to a slit in response. Or I simply may be following
an impulse to 'check the pastures' as I did in childhood, riding shotgun
in the old pick-up next to Dad. I'd slide over the stick and 'drive through'
when he muscled the barbed wire gates open and then afterward closed.

I abandon the eroded two- track about to high-center my Subaru
to drive cross country. Up a rough hill dodging prickly pear, I notice
even late in October, the persistence of tiny green blades of grass.
I'm lost in a patch of big bluestem but the crest of the hill pulls me up
with a longing for the long view across the river. With a sudden taste of sage
I top out, startled as the big rocks erupt into windshield view.
The familiar outcrop has grown striking in my absence. Aggregate granite
grays glow purple in the lengthening light, lime lichen spots and spirals.

It's been exactly five years since we scattered Dad. Exact because of the plaque
Walt and Eddie attached to a shed-sized face of stone. Cows have loafed
and left their flops on the sand embedding the rocks. Grains of sand shift
even now in the ever-present wind, reveal an arrowhead—still pointing
toward the shadow of those who not long ago sheltered onsite.

I take a seat on the ground near my father's plaque—warm stone on my back,
sun on my face. I close my eyes to the glare with regret because I enjoy
the choreography in front of me, the waving and bowing, genuflecting stems
of golden sandhill grass.   But I came to listen.   So, listen.

Far-off a truck jake-brakes getting off the interstate.

What do I expect?   my father to speak?
to say ... *it's OK—you didn't turn out so bad after all...*

Horned larks twitter. Switchgrass rattles. My mammalian memory rests,
forever done with the review of snits and rages, the pithy phrases
of cowboy wisdom listed on Dad's funeral flyer.

An enduring beat of blood rouses. I may have fallen into the first circle of sleep.

I get to my feet grateful for a few moments acknowledging how right is our place.

When We Were Horses

Tumbleweed-tangled forelock,
cockle-burr knotted tail, born
to the prairie, we lived
on the rough. Wind whistled rhyme
into our language, hooves beat
time on packed-sand drums.

When we were horses, we'd dodge
what would catch us. On legs
like wound springs, we'd break away,
fly, our hearts like wings over
mounds of grass-grown ground.

The places we worshipped were
wide-open spaces; we bowed
our heads to green creeds of soil.
On sun-scorched afternoons, we'd
lean into one another, swing our tails
in rhythm with an orchestra of flies.

Beneath nights streaming
untethered legends of light,
we'd stand sleeping, keeping
the peace of invisible relations
between us and every other thing.

Night Story
—after Jean Valentine

Looking back at me from his death,
from the murkiest of the side-by-side motel room beds,
Father asks can he borrow my pen.

The next interval (it seemed like a long one)
is color-blur—and to no-one's surprise
we lose track of each other on the midway.

When I return to the room to pack, his bed
has been straightened,
a finger of light points out a bundle—papers

folded into a leather sleeve
tied like a gift with a leather thong,
my pen (it was an excellent pen) clipped to the top.

I knew then he'd gone ahead. But he felt closer
to me than I am to myself.
Indescribable, coded in silence, his voice
closer to me than I am to myself.

Now I see I have what I once longed for,
the one I wanted to be is the one I am.

How I Would Paint the Future
—for Lisel Mueller

I crunch through crisp snow, leave a lilac tread,
out to count birds on the first day of the year.
Clouds frost the morning with a sheen of iced pearls,
birds sit and flit through the needlework of the pines.

Entranced by branching, I see each tree as discrete,
yet, on every side, dynamically entwined.
From the corner of my eye, a sunbeam highlights
someone lifting a candelabra—No—no, no—

it's the rack of a proud bull elk! Ah! the moment—
beholding the other—dissolves into dreamwork
when he turns.   As I turn I picture an image—
a figure, seen from the back, casting a shadow
forward across a field of unmarked snow.

IN APPRECIATION

My heartfelt thanks to my teachers and mentors at Lighthouse Writers Workshop, especially John Brehm, the late Chris Ransick, Elizabeth Robinson, and Andrea Rexilius for guidance at Lit Fest, in the Poetry Book Project and through the Poetry Collective.

Thank you, Voices of Women: Laurie Bogue, the late Peggy Dinkel, Michelle Gallegos, Joan Hershberger and our leader, Barbara Ittner for decades of collective poetic engagement.

Love and gratitude to all my fellow writers and readers, especially Diane Alters, Gail ben Ezra, Lois Levinson, Kirsten Morgan, Erika Walker, and Connie Zumpf, a steadfast council with whom poetry becomes a bond and a gift.

Harriet Stratton's work has appeared in *Pilgrimage Magazine, Windward Review* and among other publications, *Passager Journal.* "While Making Fence with My Father" was featured in their *Burning Bright* podcast on Father's Day, 2022. Her work is anthologized in *An Uncertain Age, Poems by Bold Women of a Certain Age* (Ink Sisters Press, 2021) and *Rumors, Secrets & Lies, Poems About Pregnancy, Abortion & Choice* (Anhinga Press, 2022). The editors of Anhinga Press nominated Harriet's poem, "*Caught in Amber*" for a 2023 Pushcart Prize.
This is her first chapbook.

Harriet lives and writes atop a red rock butte in Perry Park, Colorado. A longtime member of Denver's Lighthouse Writer's Workshop, she graduated from the Poetry Book Project and remains a member of the Poetry Collective. Formally educated in Design and Art Education, Stratton practiced what she taught—painting, drawing and printmaking—in a 25-year teaching career.

Poems in *Ear to the Ground* remember Stratton's father and mother and draw from the lifestyle that like an album of fading snapshots backgrounds her upbringing on a Colorado cattle ranch. There she learned to remember. Traces of what's been forgot lead her current interest in prehistory's language—pictures carved and painted on stone. Because the past beckons us toward understanding, she strives to interpret the code.

www.ingramcontent.com/pod-product-compliance
Lightning Source LLC
Chambersburg PA
CBHW020224090426
42734CB00008B/1212